Honey

Khalid Elhawary

SHE SAID TO ME

Where world are you from?

And with any magic did you come!

And any saying you said

You spoke with me, and I heard

You asked me, and I answered

You ordered me, and I obeyed

Whispered to me

Fascinated me

Numb your speech when you say it

You hijacked all my feelings

And you passed all my crossings

You tore me in silence

I closed my heart before

For all kinds of love

How did you get me?

I prevented myself from

The futility of love

You came to me

And you raid me over

And over again

You receive me with passion

I lost my Reflections

I see you my evening and my present

And literal melts in my mouth

And my heart wanders

In your endless streets

I fell in love

I no longer have power

Because you are straining me

And longing overcomes me

You did you do me

Where world are you from?

Earlier when we were young

We were neighbors on the farm

We run among the fields

Between watercourses, and flowers

We play in the evening

And every evening

We repeat stories and singing

We grew up, slowly

Love infiltrated us

Slowly, without hassle

And was my lover liked to travel

My loved did not come

And the train did not come

I am sitting in my silence

Pass sad minutes

Shadows walk in front of me weakling

And Delusions roll over my head

As rocks

Why was the train delayed?

Why is the train late?

My lover will come

After a long wait

Heart is extinguished

And words are difficult to come

Out in such situations

Love becomes the companion of pain

(2)

?I asked you Once Do you love me

"Yes of course"

–she said it deceptively and fake –

Now Promises have been lost

I have been lost passion

I learned from you the meaning of deception

The meaning of life with the taste of tears

I see you now without mask

My soul is shattered glass

I embrace the Impossible's face

Then I unfolded into the depths of myself

I am approaching perfection

I see her as something unique

Far away Sublime above beauty.

Do you kidnapped tree branch the thinness of
your waist

He wandered inclined and persistent

You overthrow my poetry and my heart

Absent Me

I missed the light of she eyes

I increased my longing even though I

I don't know if she brusqueness me

On fondness or she deserted me

Did they tell her?

Bad news that does not return it

Do not blame me

My life was lost in this the love

I do not desire anything but my sweetheart

Gorgeous my sweetheart

Whoso cast doubts my sorrow

The tears of my heart did not leave me

She was slept at night

My eyes are watchful

She is playing with my heart

You ask her is the story ended.

Or do her   abstaining from me?

I Asking she to meet me

My face wandering in the universe

Nod the flute, increase me

Fill the cup with singing

I pour out the melody, wait for me

My thoughts are sublimated

If only she would clear

Always is the same in me

Go Away From Me

(1)

The One-sided love

Waste of time

And the folly of a person

Looking for his pain

He hopes that love will come to him

Affectionate on him, kneeling in his arms

(2)

Oh how did this love come?

I do not know

Where is his medicine?

Or is it hoped to cure?

Oh, damn this disease

This makes me tired

My heart like a wilderness

There is no water for the soul

It makes my days turn Fluctuate

Without clarity

Oh love from one −sided

Oh wolf tore my organs

Oh numb, roamed around me

Leave me, Go away

And to pack your bags from my heart

(3)

What a pity my grieving heart

The deep wound is feverish

My soul has reached the locum

The embers crumbled

O my soul in any direction

You will walk

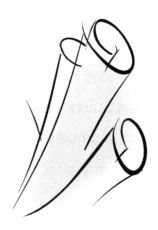

False Claims

Are you claiming?

That you do not love me?

And a day has come that you hate me

And that my heart no longer shakes you

And you pretend that you excluded me

About the throne of your heart

And I am no longer your love

Do not you claim it is my fault?

Longing in your eyes exposes what is hidden

He says that you love me

And you adore me and adore me

Your eyes are lying

And you know that you are

You have melted one day at My Love

So this is called a fake enmity

And when we met – and how much we did –

by chance

As if nothing has changed in your life

After

Love was slaughtered on your hands

She claims you have come to me to say

goodbye

Learn and to understand

So pencil my problems

If I thought so

Try to disappoint me

Or lose me

So come down, or keep going

Stubborn

And remember

The Weakness in sea of love Strength

Death on the land of love Glory

Fancy is the spectrum of insanity

If you come back one day

I am waiting for you

APPEAL

Appeal To all women

Not all men are equal

Some words are medicine

And some words like victory

And glory

And some talk is nonsense

And some souls are pure

And some souls are misery

An appeal to all women

Don't mix men's words with water

And drink from it

This is not quenching

Some men's hearts are like Flimsy crust

And some men's hearts are like eagles

And some hearts are air

An appeal all women

Do not shoot arrows from your eyes

Haphazardly

DELIRIUM

Thirsty

Still a Young Girl

You're still a Young girl

Are you searching for passion?

Are you searching and asking

And you enter the love poems

Without asking permission

And you claim that the Youth are all

They have left the covenant of love

Since years

You denounce and request

The Knight of Dreams is loved

Coming above his horse

From the ages of the Lovers

You're still a Young girl

Do not be in a hurry

Do not go into seas of love

Sailing in the high wave snappy

You will drown

You're still a Young girl

Do not rush

Oh flower

Between Girls garden

One day the cloud of love will come to you

Laden with eagerness rain

Love will fall on your forehead

You're still a Young girl

Do not rush

Love will come to you

Even after a while

Sinbad

Be spoiled, hey my girl and sway and look
forward

You are my love

I was read the books of poetry from

Beginning to end

I couldn't find poems that could describe you

If I lost a day

My map is you

I will fight to horrors and dangers

Till I see you

If I ever return, my seasons are you

My free bird

And a celestial star

You are my marina and my refuge

Oh My Charmer

some talk ،Love will not be

And Poems embroidered with colors

Of dreams

Love is great situations

Major battles without surrender

So go deep in love with gently

And Leave your innocent childish fanaticism

Leave the contrived quarrel

My girl you is still brilliant

Do not be in a hurry

I find it in every way

Spectra of candles

I need love

He gives me a secret of secrets

Makes me dance in fun

Like kids

I see it as a green scarf

Without holes

As a hidden fairy city

Without paths

Love blooms like flowers

Star twinkling

In every orbit

A bird sings and sings

Stony girl

Her heart is a stone

And If I try to love her

This is dangerous

Very dangerous

The moon saw her

He got angry and apologized

And leave staying up

So I said, sweetheart

She is moon

Love her, if you know

Since ever

When I see her

I feel like a kid dancing in the rain

And when she smiles

What a smile, beyond extravaganza

They said to me

Why do you love faraway moon

And a stony heart ?

I said for them

Perhaps

A fountain of water

Flowing from it

Part of the journey is over

Dear sailor

And life goes on